Scott Foresman

Ten Important Sentences

PEARSON
Scott Foresman

Editorial Offices: Glenview, Illinois • Parsippany, New Jersey • New York, New York
Sales Offices: Needham, Massachusetts • Duluth, Georgia • Glenview, Illinois
Coppell, Texas • Sacramento, California • Mesa, Arizona

ISBN: 0-328-16905-6

Contents

Unit 1:   Meeting Challenges

Unit 2:   Doing the Right Thing

Unit 3:   Inventors and Artists

Why Are Sentences So Important?

The sentence is the basic means of written communication. In order to be literate and articulate, students need to master sentence power.

When students read, they get information from sentences. Sentences provide facts and details, opinions, clues about the sequence of events, and information to understand cause and effect relationships. Students cannot get such meaning from sounds or words alone. Readers use sentences to build meaning in context and to decide on a main idea. You can think of the steps to comprehension as an inverted triangle, illustrating that comprehension is built upon the understanding that sounds create words that are parts of sentences which make up a text.

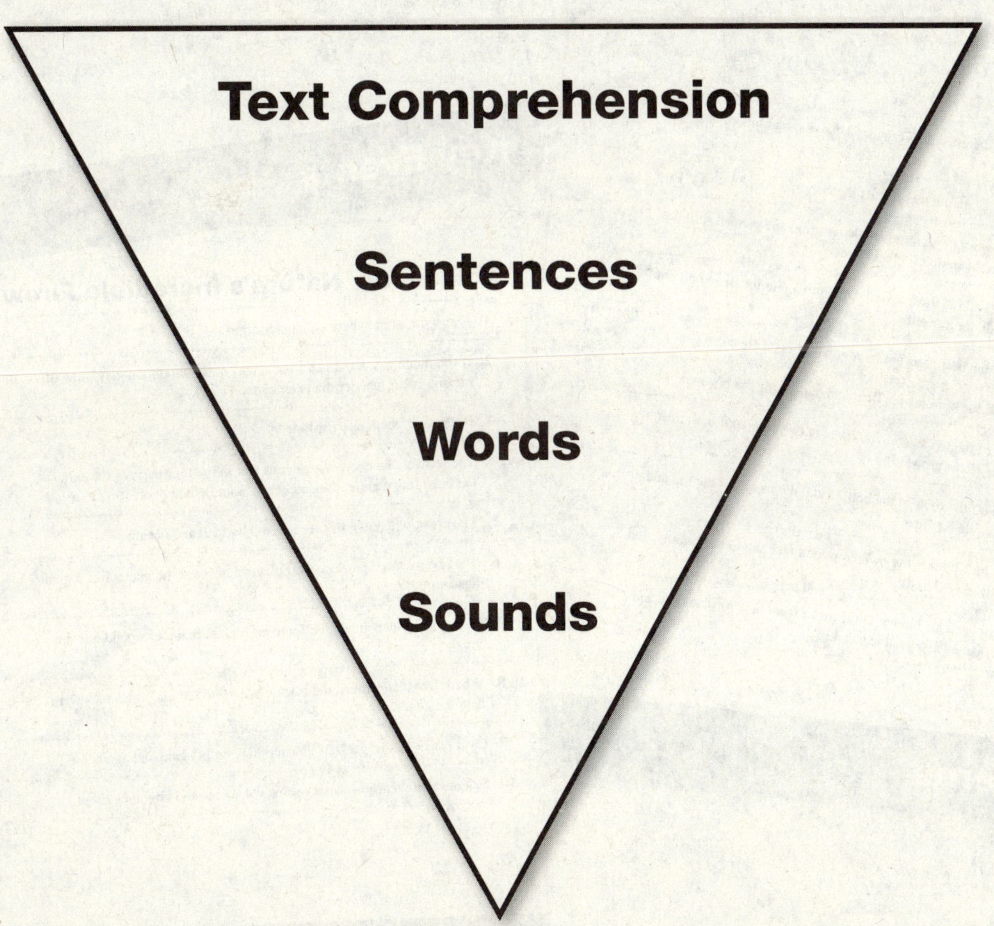

In this booklet, Ten Important Sentences are provided for every selection in the Student Edition. Each sentence is logical and cohesive; each sentence provides a key idea from the selection. Together, the Ten Important Sentences help students make meaning in several ways. Depending on the genre, Ten Important Sentences can do any of the following:

- Present **key events** in a story or narrative nonfiction selection such as a biography or autobiography

- Give the stated **main ideas and details** in an essay or informational selection, or

- Demonstrate a predictable **pattern** in a selection, for example in a song, poem, or nonsense story

Gertrude Ederle

1. Gertrude Ederle was born on October 23, 1906.
2. She loved to swim.
3. By 1925 Trudy had set twenty-nine U.S. and world records.
4. She was determined to take on the ultimate challenge: the English Channel.
5. A newspaper editorial declared that Trudy wouldn't make it and that women must admit they would "remain forever the weaker sex."
6. She knew she would either swim the Channel or drown.
7. At about nine-forty at night, after more than fourteen hours in the water, Trudy's feet touched land.
8. She beat the men's record by almost two hours.
9. Reporters declared that the myth that women are the weaker sex was "shattered and shattered forever."
10. Gertrude Ederle had become a beacon of strength to girls and women everywhere.

Key Events

Tops & Bottoms

1. Once upon a time there lived a very lazy bear who had lots of money and lots of land.
2. So Hare and Mrs. Hare put their heads together and cooked up a plan.
3. "I'll do the hard work of planting and harvesting, and we can split the profit right down the middle," (said Hare).
4. Hare plucked off all the tops, tossed them into a pile for Bear, and put the bottoms aside for himself.
5. "But, Hare, all the best parts are in your half!" (said Bear).
6. Hare pulled off the bottoms for Bear and put the tops in his own pile.
7. "You've tricked me twice, and you owe me one season of both tops and bottoms!" (Bear growled).
8. Hare tugged off the roots at the bottom and the tassels at the top and put them in a pile for Bear.
9. "From now on I'll plant my own crops and take the tops, bottoms, and middles!" (Bear hollered).
10. Hare bought back his land with the profit from the crops, and he and Mrs. Hare opened a vegetable stand.

Patterns

Volcanoes: Nature's Incredible Fireworks

1. Every day somewhere volcanoes erupt.
2. If too much gas is trapped inside, part of the mountain may blow off, hurling rocks heavier than elephants for miles.
3. But not all volcanoes explode.
4. The answers lie deep beneath our feet in the four parts of the earth— the crust, the mantle, the outer core, and the inner core.
5. The crust, where we live, is covered by land and oceans.
6. It is several large pieces called plates that cover the planet like a giant jigsaw puzzle.
7. Where two plates meet, the force is so great that rocks bend or even break.
8. Where two plates meet, the mantle grows hotter, and volcanoes form near the edges.
9. Over thousands of years, a volcano may erupt again and again.
10. Scientists are learning what causes volcanoes and how they erupt.

Main Ideas and Details

How Ten Important Sentences Build Comprehension

Using and reusing *Ten Important Sentences* helps students build the skills they need for comprehension. *Ten Important Sentences* provides practical, selection-based instruction in these important skills:

- Recalling facts and details

- Finding and distinguishing between facts and opinions

- Arranging events in sequence

- Recognizing cause and effect relationships

- Identifying main idea and supporting details

You can help your students build their sentence power. Try these activities for building sentence power using *Ten Important Sentences*. The examples shown are from Grade 3. Match activities with other selections as you see fit.

Activity 1: Locate Sentences

1. Read the selection aloud to students or have students read all or parts of the selection silently.

2. Have students locate each of the Ten Important Sentences. (These will be those that tell the story or present the important ideas and details of the selection. The sentences on each master are in the correct order.) Discuss whether students agree with the choice of sentences. Which could they add or delete?

Activity 2: Distinguish Facts and Opinions

1. Read the selection aloud to students or have the students read all or parts
of the selection silently. Discuss the selection, emphasizing sentences that
are facts and sentences that are opinions.

2. Have students mark each of the Ten Important Sentences "F" for fact
(something that can be proven) or "O" for opinion (something that a
person believes or feels).

Me and Uncle Romie

1. Daddy thought it was a good time for me (James) to visit Uncle Romie and his wife, Aunt Nanette, up north in New York City.   **F**

2. No, I wasn't sure about this visit at all.   **O**

3. Home was like nothing I'd ever seen before.   **O**

4. "Your uncle's working very hard, so we won't see much of him for a while" (said Aunt Nanette).   **F**

5. My birthday was ruined.   **O**

6. Looking at Uncle Romie's paintings, I could feel Harlem—its beat and bounce.   **O**

7. "But the things we care about are pretty much the same" (said Uncle Romie).   **O**

8. Uncle Romie held up two tickets to a baseball game!   **F**

9. All these strangers talking to each other about their families and friends and special times, and all because of how my Uncle Romie's painting reminded them of things.   **F**

10. And then I was off on a treasure hunt, collecting things that reminded me of Uncle Romie.   **F**

Activity 3: Sequence Events

1. Read the selection aloud to students or have students read all or parts of the selection silently. Discuss the sequence of events, thoughts, or ideas in the selection.

2. Have students cut apart the Ten Important Sentences and mix the sentences in random order. Then have students order them correctly. (Note: Students can work with the sentences numbered or not, as you wish.)

Sequence
We all got together to build a church and a school.
Now this was a real boom town!

Activity 4: Link Cause and Effect

1. Read the selection aloud to students or have students read all or parts of the selection silently. Talk about events in the story and what causes them to happen.

2. Have students look at the Ten Important Sentences and find one or more pairs of sentences in which one sentence tells what happens and the other tells why it happens.

Cause
"There is more snow here than at home in England," said William.

Effect
He built a new roof with a very steep pitch and replaced the shingles.

ix

Activity 5: Determine Main Idea

1. After reading, focus on the selection and talk with students about the big ideas.

2. Have students locate the sentences that provide the five elements of the main idea: who? did what? where? when? and why? Help students as they write the answers to these important questions in one sentence of their own.

Every day somewhere volcanoes erupt.

Notice that over time, students listen, manipulate sentences, and draw conclusions as they work toward comprehending what they have read. Using the Ten Important Sentences frees you from creating worksheets and lets you concentrate on helping students read and write with confidence.

x

The Main Idea Glove

Use the main idea glove to talk about the five elements of main idea. Duplicate this outline for each child or post it in your classroom. Your student will have the main idea right at hand!

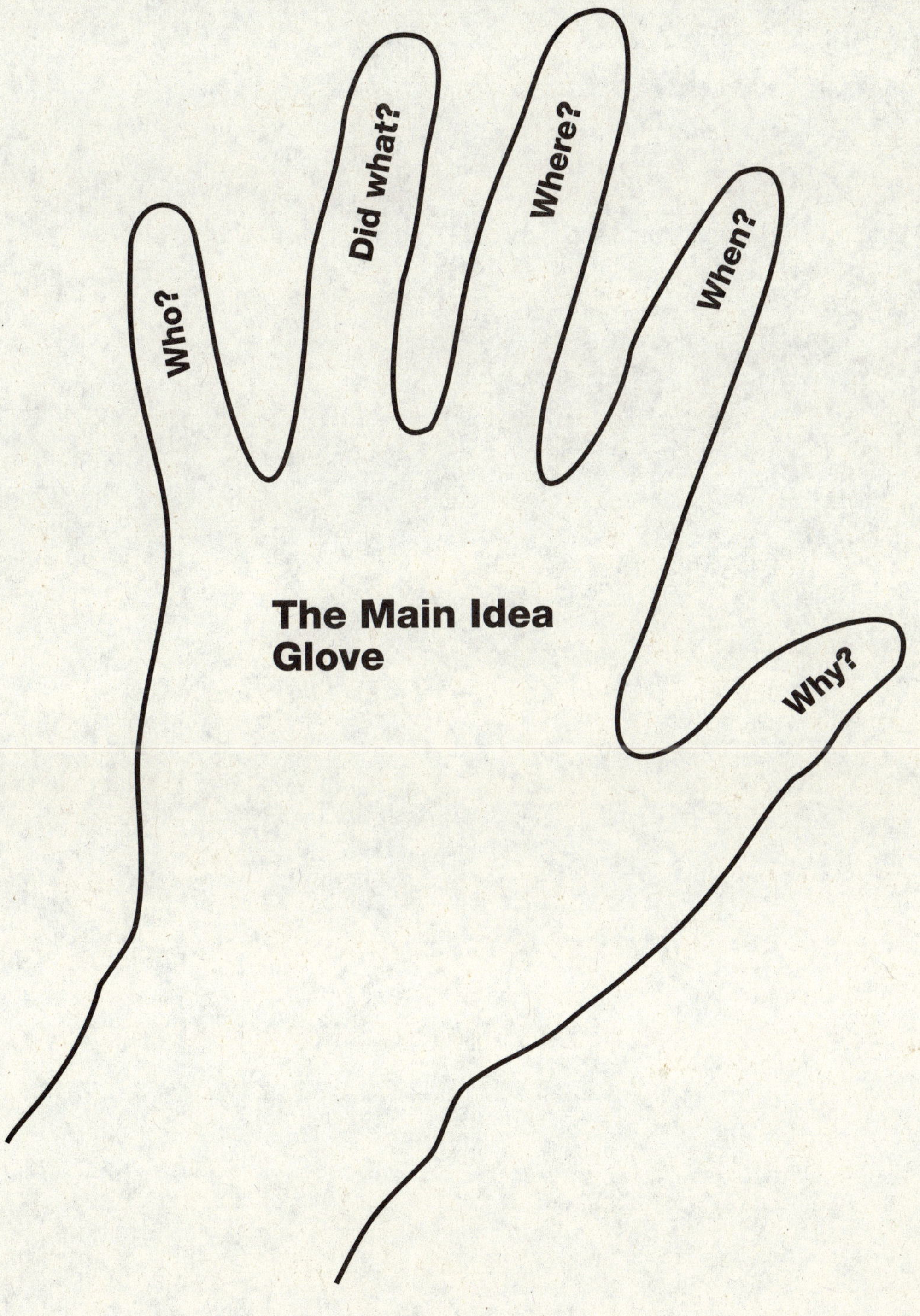

Frindle

1. Everyone was sure that Mrs. Granger had X-ray vision.

2. All the kids at Lincoln Elementary School knew that at the end of the line—fifth grade—Mrs. Granger would be the one grading their spelling tests and their reading tests, and worst of all, their vocabulary tests—week after week, month after month.

3. But he (Nick) figured that he got all the words he needed just by reading, and he read all the time.

4. It was still a week before school and Nick already felt like fifth grade was going to be a very long year.

5. Nick was an expert at asking the delaying question—also known as the teacher-stopper, or the guaranteed-time-waster.

6. Here he was in fifth grade, near the end of his very first language arts class with Mrs. Granger, and Nick could feel a homework assignment coming the way a farmer can feel a rainstorm.

7. Nick was famous for this, and the whole class knew what he was doing.

8. Unfortunately, so did Mrs. Granger.

9. A complete shutdown.

10. Everything he (Nick) had heard about this teacher was true—don't mess around with The Lone Granger.

Thunder Rose

1. Hailing rain, flashing lightning, and booming thunder pounded the door, inviting themselves in for the blessed event.

2. She (the infant) took ahold of that lightning, rolled it into a ball, and set it above her shoulder, while the thunder echoed out over the other.

3. Overcome with that love, they (ma and pa) lifted their voices in song, an old song and a melody so sweet and true—a lullaby passed down from the ages, echoing since the beginning of time.

4. "I'll register it here at the bull's-eye set in the center of my heart, and see what I can do with it one day!" (said Rose).

5. And true to her word, Rose did *more* than grow good and strong.

6. She (Rose) constructed a thunderbolt as black as pitch to punctuate her name.

7. The mighty sun was draining the moisture out of every living thing it touched.

8. Suddenly a rotating column of air came whirling and swirling around, picking up everything in its path.

9. Oh, this riled Rose so much, she became the only two-legged tempest to walk the western plains.

10. And Rose realized that by reaching into her own heart to bring forth the music that was there, she had even touched the hearts of the clouds.

Island of the Blue Dolphins

1. But even if they (the white men) came soon, before next summer, I could not live without a roof or a place to store my food.

2. I needed a place that was sheltered from the wind, not too far from Coral Cove, and close to a good spring.

3. The thing that made me decide on the place to build my house was the sea elephants.

4. I put the ribs together with their edges almost touching, and standing so that they curved outward, which made them impossible to climb.

5. I built the fence first because it was too cold to sleep on the rock, and I did not like to sleep in the shelter I had made until I was safe from the wild dogs.

6. The winter was half over before I finished the house, but I slept there every night and felt secure because of the strong fence.

7. While I was building the fence and the house, I ate shellfish and perch which I cooked on a flat rock.

8. For cooking seeds and roots I wove a tight basket of fine reeds, which was easy because I had learned how to do it from my sister Ulape.

9. These (cracks) I cut out and smoothed to make shelves where I could store my food and the mice could not reach it.

10. Everything I wanted was there at hand.

Satchel Paige

----

1. He'd pick up a tip here and there, put his Satchel spin on it, and polish it off with a brand-new name.

----

2. Folks would pack the stands to see how many Satchel could strike out in one game.

----

3. The more cheers he heard, the more his confidence grew.

----

4. Because the white major-league ball clubs wouldn't allow blacks to play in their leagues, blacks had created their own in 1920 and named them the Negro Leagues.

----

5. Negro League players were often refused meals in restaurants and rooms in hotels.

----

6. Once he reached his mid-thirties, the joys of traveling began to wear thin for Satchel.

----

7. But even though he had finally found what he thought he'd been searching for, it was only a year before he took to the road again with his first and only true love—baseball.

----

8. Because of his powerful hitting and home run record, Josh was sometimes called "the black Babe Ruth," but many wondered if the Babe should have been called "the white Josh Gibson."

----

9. "Someday we'll meet up and see who's best" rang in Satch's ears as he prepared to face the man who would now determine the fate of his team and Satch's reputation.

----

10. "Nobody hits Satchel's fastball," he said through a smile as bright as the sun.

Shutting Out the Sky

1. One early morning in December 1900, a sixteen-year-old boy left Ellis Island and made his way alone into New York City.

2. Before long, Marcus found himself in the apartment of the Segal family, who had arrived from Romania just three months before.

3. That evening, people Marcus had never seen before began to stream into the apartment, tired from a long day of work.

4. Back home in his village only rich people could indulge in the luxury of meat in the middle of the day, eat such extraordinary vegetables, use soap instead of sand to clean floors, or live on the second floor of such a nice apartment.

5. To a newcomer, or "greenhorn," like Marcus, it was all very confusing.

6. Mrs. Segal gave Marcus a dollar and pushed him out onto the street to get started as a peddler.

7. This certainly wasn't the way he'd imagined his start in America.

8. Now he was in business.

9. As it happened, the man was also from Romania, and he took Marcus under his wing.

10. Marcus was on his way.

Inside Out

1. Curtis was the biggest, strongest, and most popular kid in the class.

2. I preferred to hang around Arthur, one of the boys who knew a little Spanish.

3. I knew caterpillars turned into butterflies because Roberto had told me, but I wanted to know more.

4. I drew all kinds of animals but mostly birds and butterflies.

5. The next day I was on the playground wearing my new jacket and waiting for the first bell to ring when I saw Curtis coming at me like an angry bull.

6. For the rest of the day, I could not even pretend I was paying attention to Miss Scalapino; I was so embarrassed.

7. I did not understand what she said, but I heard her say my name as she held up a blue ribbon.

8. For the next several minutes we all stood there watching the butterfly emerge from its cocoon, in slow motion.

9. Curtis motioned for me to show him the drawing again.

10. "It's yours," I repeated, handing the drawing to Curtis.

Passage to Freedom

- -

1. Then one early morning in late July, my life changed forever.

- -

2. Outside, I saw hundreds of people crowded around the gate in front of our house.

- -

3. These people were refugees—people who ran away from their homes because, if they stayed, they would be killed.

- -

4. He (father) said the refugees needed his help, that they needed permission from him to go to another part of the world where they would be safe.

- -

5. "I may have to disobey my government, but if I don't, I will be disobeying my conscience," (said father).

- -

6. They said we had to think about the people outside before we thought about ourselves.

- -

7. With the entire family in agreement, I could tell a huge weight was lifted off my father's shoulders.

- -

8. "I will issue visas to each and every one of you to the last," (said father).

- -

9. My mother offered to help write the visas, but my father insisted he be the only one, so no one else could get into trouble.

- -

10. The people in the front of the crowd looked into my father's eyes and cried, " We will never forget you!"

- -

The Ch'i-lin Purse

1. Although Hsiang-ling was spoiled, she was not a mean-spirited person.

2. She realized that she was lucky to have so many things, while this girl had nothing.

3. Hsiang-ling had given away her mother's wedding gift without ever finding out what was inside.

4. In a year's time, when she became the mother of a little boy, she felt she was the happiest woman in the world.

5. But six years later, there came a terrible flood.

6. So Hsiang-ling began her life as a governess.

7. But in the place where people usually put the wooden name-tablets of their ancestors was the Ch'i-lin Purse!

8. Mrs. Lu dropped to her knees in front of Hsiang-ling and cried, "You are my benefactor!"

9. "We shall divide our property and give you half of it," (said Mrs. Lu).

10. Later, whenever Hsiang-ling told people about her purse, she would always end the tale by saying, "If you have a chance to do something good, be sure to do it."

Jane Goodall's 10 Ways to Help Save Wildlife

1. Respect all life.

2. Think of animals as individuals.

3. Dare to admit that humans aren't the only thinking, feeling beings on the planet.

4. Get to know animals.

5. Be willing to learn from animals.

6. Speak up for what you believe.

7. Use less paper, gasoline, and red meat.

8. Be inspired by the work of others.

9. Join Roots & Shoots.

10. Have hope.

The Midnight Ride of Paul Revere

1. Listen, my children, and you shall hear/ Of the midnight ride of Paul Revere,/ On the eighteenth of April, in Seventy-Five,/ Hardly a man is now alive/ Who remembers that famous day and year.

2. He said to his friend, "If the British march/ By land or by sea from the town tonight,/ Hang a lantern aloft in the belfry arch/ Of the North Church tower as a signal light—/One, if by land, and two, if by sea;/ And I on the opposite shore will be,/ Ready to ride and spread the alarm/ Through every Middlesex village and farm,/ For the country folk to be up and to arm."

3. And lo! as he looks, on the belfry's height/ A glimmer, and then a gleam of light!

4. And yet, through the gloom and the light,/ The fate of a nation was riding that night;/ And the spark struck out by that steed, in his flight,/ Kindled the land into flame with its heat.

5. It was twelve by the village clock,/When he crossed the bridge into Medford town.

6. It was one by the village clock,/ When he galloped into Lexington.

7. It was two by the village clock,/When he came to the bridge in Concord town.

8. And one was safe and asleep in his bed/ Who at the bridge would be first to fall,/ Who that day would be lying dead,/ Pierced by a British musket-ball.

9. In the books you have read/ How the British Regulars fired and fled—/ How the farmers gave them ball for ball,/ From behind each fence and farmyard wall,/ Chasing the red-coats down the lane,/ Then crossing the fields to emerge again/ Under the trees at the turn of the road/ And only pausing to fire and load.

10. So through the night rode Paul Revere,/ And so through the night went his cry of alarm/ To every Middlesex village and farm—/ A cry of defiance and not of fear,/ A voice in the darkness, a knock at the door,/ And a word that shall echo for evermore!

Wings for the King

----

1. **KING** My darling, my life lacks adventure.

----

2. **KING** I want to fly!

----

3. **KING** I will give that bag of gold to the person who brings me a pair of wings that will help me fly.

----

4. **PAGE** Sire, may I present your loyal subject, Tina Applewhite, and her, uh, wings.

----

5. **QUEEN** My beloved, would you please give up this dangerous business before you get yourself killed?.

----

6. **ISAAC** Your Majesties, may I present the best wings of all!

----

7. **ISAAC** You don't wear them, Your Majesty, you look at them.

----

8. **KING** I feel as if I'm really there!

----

9. **ISAAC** Books are wings to the land of knowledge.

----

10. **KING** With books around, I don't think I'll ever be bored again.

Leonardo's Horse

1. For a man who liked to ask questions, Leonardo da Vinci was born at the right time—April 15, 1452.

2. He had heard that the duke of Milan wanted to honor his father with a bronze horse in front of his palace.

3. He measured and drew pictures until he knew where all the bones and muscles of a horse were.

4. The hardest part would be the casting.

5. In November 1493, he had completed the clay model—twenty-four feet high.

6. Later, in 1498, there were rumors that the French were preparing to invade Milan, and the duke wanted to be ready.

7. At last it was nothing but a pile of mud stuck with arrows.

8. Leonardo went back to inventing and painting, but he never forgot his horse.

9. On May 2, 1519, Leonardo da Vinci died.

10. It was said that even on his deathbed, Leonardo wept for his horse.

The Dinosaurs of Waterhouse Hawkins

1. Even though the English had found the first known dinosaur fossil many years before—and the bones of more dinosaurs had been unearthed in England since then—in 1853, most people had no idea what a dinosaur looked like.

2. He wanted to create such perfect models that anyone—a crowd of curious children, England's leading scientists, even the Queen herself! —could gaze at his dinosaurs and see into the past.

3. Waterhouse pointed out that the few iguanodon bones helped determine the model's size and proportion.

4. While Richard Owen could imagine their shapes, it took an artist to bring the animals to life.

5. Waterhouse showed his guests the small models he'd made, correct in every detail, from scales on the nose to nails on the toes.

6. With the help of his assistants, he had formed the life-size clay figures and created the molds from them.

7. Then he erected iron skeletons, built brick foundations, and covered the whole thing with cement casts from the dinosaur-shaped molds.

8. But he would soon face a much tougher set of critics: England's leading scientists.

9. All the guests agreed: The iguanodon was a marvelous success.

10. Forty thousand spectators attended the regal ceremony.

Mahalia Jackson

----

1. The words of a blues song might be sad, but the music and the beat wrap around your heart like one of your grandmother's hugs.

----

2. The roots of the blues go back to slavery.

----

3. They wove hope on the air by singing songs called spirituals—songs for the spirit.

----

4. She sang church songs, gospel, but she knew blues and brought the blues feeling into church music.

----

5. Mahalia grew up in New Orleans, Louisiana, the city where jazz was born and where there is still more good music and good food per block than anyplace in the world.

----

6. Mahalia grew up loving music, and the person she wanted to sing like was none other than Bessie Smith.

----

7. It was in church that Mahalia first started singing.

----

8. Mahalia's singing brought her to the attention of Thomas A. Dorsey, who directed a number of gospel choirs in Chicago.

----

9. He began taking her to out-of-town churches for concerts and her reputation began to grow almost as fast as you are.

----

10. She would go on to become the most famous gospel singer in the world, and in 1976 she received (posthumously) a Grammy Lifetime Achievement Award.

Special Effects in Film and Television

1. The art of miniature model-making has always been an important part of special effects in movies.

2. A special effects team must build a prehistoric world in a workshop.

3. The movie makers study this concept model to decide on the size and shape of the finished product.

4. Model-makers carve the plastic surface to make hills and valleys and rivers and lakes.

5. The model is cut into sections so it can be taken on trucks to the television studio.

6. At the studio, the model is put back together, and the miniature trees, rocks, and other surface details are all put in place.

7. Many future movies will be created or enhanced on screen, using computer generated imagery (CGI).

8. The model-makers go to great lengths to make a miniature look as realistic as possible.

9. It has taken most of the day to reassemble the entire miniature landscape.

10. The large painted backdrop and studio lighting add to the effect of a vast prehistoric landscape roamed by early reptiles.

Weslandia

1. He (Wesley) was an outcast from the civilization around him.

2. He (Wesley) would grow his own staple food crop—and found his own civilization!

3. Wesley found it thrilling to open his land to chance, to invite the new and unknown.

4. Ignoring the shelf of cereals in the kitchen, Wesley took to breakfasting on the fruit.

5. To keep off the sun, Wesley wove himself a hat from strips of the plant's woody bark.

6. His domain, home to many such innovations, he named "Weslandia."

7. Uninterested in traditional sports, Wesley made up his own.

8. In like manner, he'd named his new fabrics, games, and foods, until he'd created an entire language.

9. As the finale to his summer project, he used the ink and his own eighty-letter alphabet to record the history of his civilization's founding.

10. He had no shortage of friends.

Stretching Ourselves

1. Emily has cerebral palsy (CP).

2. The brain controls how we move, speak, see, smell, hear, and learn.

3. Because the muscles and tendons in her legs are tight, Emily's movements are stiff and she walks slightly bent forward.

4. Tasks that are simple for most people can be big challenges for people with CP.

5. He (Nic) spends most of his time in a wheelchair and can speak only a few words.

6. Tanner has milder CP than Nic or Emily, and many people don't notice his limp or his weak left arm.

7. People with CP *are* brave.

8. Adults with CP work at many different jobs.

9. Having CP means working hard at simple things.

10. "We like the same things you like," (says Emily).

Exploding Ants

----

1. By stretching, swelling, and bursting open, they can trick predators, store food, swallow big gulps, and defend their nests.

----

2. Repletes spend their lives hanging upside down from the roof of their nest waiting to feed or be fed.

----

3. Their bodies provide sterile, airtight food containers.

----

4. As they take in more and more food, the repletes swell.

----

5. Soldier ants of the species *Camponotus saundersi* are designed to explode.

----

6. When the ants explode, they spray out a sticky chemical that kills or glues their opponents in place.

----

7. Every evening before it goes off to hunt, an owl spits up a few balls of fur and bones.

----

8. Owls normally spit up two pellets a day.

----

9. The snake's ability to swallow big prey results from the special design of its jaw.

----

10. Because snakes eat such big meals, they don't need to eat every day.

The Stormi Giovanni Club

1. **STORMI** I just moved here from Chicago where I had great friends, played basketball, and was on the speech team.

2. **STORMI** From now on it's the Stormi Giovanni Club, and I'm the only member.

3. **STORMI** Lunch at a new school is the worst.

4. **AJITHA** That book is quite scintillating.

5. **HANNAH** You can sit here and read if you want to.

6. **STORMI** Lunch was almost as much fun as listening to David's lame jokes would have been.

7. **STORMI** You can't know when you will stop missing the last place so much it hurts, but you can't stop tying your shoes either.

8. **STORMI** It's silly, but I thought I would feel better if I didn't make friends.

9. **STORMI** I felt worse and I think people thought I was mean.

10. **STORMI** So, I've decided to let other members into the Stormi Giovanni Club.

The Gymnast

1. For three days of my eleventh summer I listened to my mother yap about my cousin, Isaac, who was taking gymnastics.

2. I was jealous because I had watched my share of *Wide World of Sports* and knew that people admired an athlete who could somersault without hurting himself.

3. My cousin was a showoff, but I figured he was allowed the limelight before one appreciative dog who had come over to look.

4. I went to the front yard with my wrists dripping tape and my hands white as gloves.

5. But when I did a cartwheel, the shoes flew off, along with the tape, and my cousin yelled and stomped the grass.

6. I was jealous and miserable, but the next day I found a pair of old vinyl slippers in the closet that were sort of like gymnastic shoes.

7. I dipped my hands in flour to keep them dry and went back outside to do cartwheels and, finally, after much hesitation, a back flip that nearly cost me my life when I landed on my head.

8. I'm taking gymnastics, I lied, and these are the kind of shoes you wear.

9. I lay on the grass, tired and sweaty, my feet squeezed in the vise of cruel slippers.

10. I ate a plum and pictured my cousin, who was probably cartwheeling to the audience of one sleeping dog.

The Three-Century Woman

1. We were heading for Whispering Oaks to see my Great-Grandmother Breckenridge, who's lived there since I was a little girl.

2. The reason for Great-Grandma's fame is that she was born in 1899.

3. When we got to her (Great Grandma's) wing, the hall was full of camera crews and a woman from the suburban newspaper with a notepad.

4. Mom and I went in first, and our eyes popped.

5. A tiny smile played around Great-Grandma's wrinkled lips.

6. Mom moaned, and the cameraman was practically standing on his head for a close-up.

7. "In your sensational span of years you've survived two great disasters!" (the anchor said).

8. "It was that TV dude in the five-hundred-dollar suit who set me off," Great-Grandma said.

9. "He thought I was nothing but my memories," (said Great-Grandma).

10. Then she hunched up her little pink shoulders and winked at me.

The Unsinkable Wreck of the R.M.S. *Titanic*

1. Inside the cramped submarine, all I could hear was the steady pinging of the sonar and the regular breathing of the pilot and engineer.

2. Like a ghost from the ancient past, the bow of the Royal Mail Steamer *Titanic,* the greatest shipwreck of all time, materialized out my viewport.

3. It was here that First Officer William Murdoch, desperate to avoid the mountain of ice that lay in the *Titanic's* path, shouted to the helmsman, "Hard a-starboard!"

4. Thirty minutes later, after learning how quickly water was pouring into the ship, he knew that the "unsinkable" *Titanic* was doomed.

5. In my mind's eye I could see the deck surging with passengers as the crew tried to keep order during the loading of the lifeboats.

6. We already knew the ship lay in two pieces, with the stern nearly two-thousand feet (six hundred meters) away.

7. Beyond it hundreds of objects that had spilled out when the ship broke in two were lying on the ocean floor.

8. As we floated out over this debris field, I found it hard to believe that only a thin film of sediment covered plates and bottles that had lain on the bottom for seventy-four years.

9. Within a few weeks of the sinking, the corpses had been consumed by underwater creatures and their bones had been dissolved by the cold salt water.

10. We had only begun to plumb its secrets.

Talk With an Astronaut

1. My Hispanic roots come from my father's side.

2. I think that it's important for children to have a role model to see what they can grow up to be.

3. My mother influenced me the most

4. I didn't actually pursue becoming an astronaut until graduate school, when I learned about the kinds of skills NASA was looking for in potential astronauts.

5. But I never considered being an astronaut as an option because when I was growing up there were no female astronauts.

6. It wasn't until the first six female astronauts were selected in 1978 that women could even think of it as a possible career path.

7. Nothing has ever gone wrong on any of my missions, and our training helps us make sure that nothing will.

8. I was in training for three years before my first mission, which isn't that long of a wait.

9. It's good that you love math, because in order to be an astronaut, a college degree in math or a technical science is very important to have.

10. You should get involved in activities where you work closely with other people—because working closely with other people is an essential part of being an astronaut!

Journey to the Center of the Earth

1. Of course, in this continuing light, there is no night, but we are very tired.

2. The raft seems to have struck some hidden rock.

3. And then we see—and how tiny we feel!—that we are in the middle of a great circle of these creatures.

4. In their fury they appear not to have seen us.

5. And so, in a thunder of broken water, the battle begins.

6. There seem to be half a dozen monsters, or more, but the truth is there are only two!

7. Now I, and Hans, and the Professor, are gazing, from our tiny raft, at a living ichthyosaurus, rising from an ocean deep inside the Earth!

8. We crouch on the raft, expecting that any moment it will be overturned and we shall drown in that wildly disturbed sea, hundreds of miles below the surface of the Earth: far, far from the sky, trees, the blessed fresh air!

9. And then, suddenly, ichthyosaurus and plesiosaurus disappear together under the waves.

10. But bit by bit the great writhings die down, and at last the plesiosaurus lies dead on the surface.

Ghost Towns of the American West

1. Virtually every ghost town has untold stories of people who longed for a chance at a better life.

2. Although ghost towns can be found throughout the world, in the United States they are most often thought of as the mining camps, cowboy towns, and other settlements of the sprawling western frontier.

3. These communities boomed as miners sought gold, silver, copper, or other precious minerals but died out when all the ore was panned from streams or blasted from rocky tunnels.

4. Seeking pay dirt, "forty-niners" (as the prospectors came to be known) streamed into California in the first of the great American gold rushes.

5. Towns sprang up overnight.

6. If the railroad bypassed the village, it quickly became a ghost town.

7. When the railroad passed thirty miles to the west, folks moved the entire town— walls and windows, as well as sidewalks, furnishings, and goods—to the railroad tracks.

8. Over time, some towns grew into large cities, such as Denver and Phoenix, while many others were abandoned and forgotten in the desert sands or mountain snows.

9. A few people got rich, but others suffered heartbreak, hunger, and plain bad luck, then abandoned the town.

10. There may be a handful of old false-front buildings, weathered to a haunting gray, with open doorways and broken windows.

At the Beach

1. While the grown-ups unloaded the car, we eagerly jumped out and ran toward the sea, peeling off our clothes along the way.

2. "Remember, don't go too far!" Mami and Aunt Olga warned us sternly from the distance.

3. "Let's explore the reef!" I (Fernando) said.

4. "He (Javi) stepped on a sea urchin!" Mari cried.

5. He (Javi) wept and limped with every step.

6. As we got closer I realized that we would have to explain how it was that we went to the reef in the first place.

7. Not only had they believed me, but we were also going to eat Mami's tortilla!

8. How could I enjoy my food when I knew I had done something I wasn't supposed to do?

9. "You know, Fernando, anyone can make a mistake," (said Mami).

10. "Thank you for telling the truth," (said Mami).

The Mystery of Saint Matthew Island

1. When twenty-nine reindeer were released on Saint Matthew Island in 1944, the future of the herd seemed bright.

2. Then something went terribly wrong.

3. But to solve the mystery, he needed to conduct a thorough investigation.

4. With the time of death narrowed down to late winter 1963-64, Klein searched for clues about the cause of death.

5. None of the animals had fat in their bone marrow when they died.

6. This was clear evidence that the herd had starved to death.

7. The damaged plant life led Klein to suspect that the reindeer had run out of nutritious food.

8. Without predators or disease to limit its numbers, the small reindeer herd had grown quickly.

9. The reindeer ate and trampled the tundra plants and lichens faster than these could grow.

10. The mystery of the Saint Matthew Island reindeer showed that in the absence of these natural checks, a growing population eventually destroys its own environment.

King Midas and the Golden Touch

1. There once lived a very rich king called Midas who believed that nothing was more precious than gold.

2. There was only one thing that Midas loved more, and that was his daughter, Aurelia.

3. "I had thought to reward you for your kindness, but with so much gold, you must surely want for nothing," (said the stranger).

4. "The golden touch would bring me all the happiness I need," (said Midas).

5. Midas lifted a spoonful of porridge to his mouth, but as soon as the porridge touched his lips it turned into a hard golden lump.

6. His cursed touch had turned Aurelia into a lifeless statue.

7. "I would give up all the gold in the world if only my daughter were restored to me," (said Midas).

8. As soon as Midas reached the spring, he plunged in without removing even his shoes.

9. Midas made his way back to the palace, where the first thing he did was to sprinkle the water over his beloved Aurelia.

10. Joyfully, then, Midas restored all else he had transformed—except for a single rose, kept forever as a reminder of the golden touch.

The Hindenburg

1. The gas cells in the *Hindenburg* were filled with hydrogen.

2. The designers of the *Hindenburg* included all the latest safety measures in their new zeppelin.

3. His dream airship would have to fly the Atlantic with the hated swastika displayed on the tail fins.

4. On May 3, 1937, sixty-one crew members and thirty-six passengers boarded the *Hindenburg* for the flight to America.

5. It was a routine landing.

6. In thirty-two seconds, the mighty airship *Hindenburg* was a mass of flaming wreckage on the ground.

7. Amazingly, of the ninety-seven people on board, sixty-seven survived the explosion.

8. The cause of the *Hindenburg* explosion is still a mystery.

9. Zeppelins were now seen as death traps, and all interest in building more of them died with the *Hindenburg*.

10. People now fly in airplanes instead of airships.

Sweet Music in Harlem

1. "A photographer from *Highnote* magazine is coming soon," C. J. blurted out, "and Uncle Click lost his hat."

2. "Uncle Click," C.J. said, "I didn't find your hat, but I did find these."

3. He held out the watch, the handkerchief, and the bow tie.

4. Big Charlie Garlic, Mattie Dee, and Canary Alma were walking down the street toward them.

5. But they weren't alone!

6. Here were some of the greatest musicians and singers in Harlem.

7. "Your nephew drew a crowd without even blowing a note!" said Charlie Garlic.

8. "I know your birthday's not until next week," said Uncle Click, "but I wanted to give you this before all the magic of today wears off."

9. "It must have fallen in there last night when I was wrapping your present," (said Uncle Click).

10. "You know a jazzman like you is going to need a good hat," said Uncle Click as he placed the beret neatly on C. J.'s head.